IN A HURRY TO BE
HOLY

Short Devotionals for Busy People

JACK EADES

WestBow Press books may be ordered through booksellers or by contacting:

WestBow Press
A Division of Thomas Nelson
1663 Liberty Drive
Bloomington, IN 47403
www.westbowpress.com
1-(866) 928-1240

Because of the dynamic nature of the Internet, any web addresses or links contained in this book may have changed since publication and may no longer be valid. The views expressed in this work are solely those of the author and do not necessarily reflect the views of the publisher, and the publisher hereby disclaims any responsibility for them.

Any people depicted in stock imagery provided by Thinkstock are models, and such images are being used for illustrative purposes only.

ISBN: 978-1-4497-9786-7 (sc)
ISBN: 978-1-4497-9787-4 (e)

Library of Congress Control Number: 2013910688

Printed in the United States of America.

WestBow Press rev. date: 06/18/2013

That if you confess with your mouth, "Jesus is Lord," and believe in your heart that God raised him from the dead, you will be saved. For it is with your heart that you believe and are justified, and it is with your mouth that you confess and are saved.

—Romans 10:9–10 (NIV)

To my God and to my family

Acknowledgments

There are many people who have helped me in various ways to bring this book to fruition. I am grateful to the following: Eleanor Eades, MD; Maddox Eades; Hannah Eades; Andrew Wall; Brian Dennison; Johnny Harris; Curtis Lewis III; Chip McDaniel; Kim Iocovozzi; Wasil Khan,MD, PhD; Reverend Mike Ricker; Silas McCaslin, DDS; John Finley, PhD; Danny Falligant; Mac Newell; Tommy Danos; Karen Roeder; and Ido Friedman, DPM. If I have left out anyone, please accept my apology.

Introduction

Purpose
This book is for those who feel they are too busy to read the entire Bible but still want to gain exposure to each book of Bible. It is also for those who want to memorize Bible verses so they can call upon those verses immediately in times of need.

Content
This devotional book contains at least one Scripture reference from each book of the Bible.

How to Use This Guide
Select a devotional, with its corresponding Bible verse, and then read the commentary. Meditate on it, and see how you can apply it to your personal life. You may also use each devotional to help you memorize the Scripture quoted.

Translations Used
English Standard Version (ESV)
New International Version (NIV)
New English Bible (NEB)
New American Standard (NASB)
New King James Version (NKJV)
King James Version (KJV)

Photographs
Unless otherwise credited, all photographs are the work of the author.

1

Whose Money Is It, Anyway?

Mine is the silver and mine is the gold declares the Lord of hosts.
—Haggai 2:8 (NEB)

The day you die, whatever wealth you have accumulated will belong to someone else. You are entrusted with money to act as a steward of that which God has bestowed on you. After all, money is only good for that which can be done with it; intrinsically, it has no value.

What are you doing with the money with which you have been entrusted?

Photograph courtesy of Curtis Lewis III

2

Pay What You Owe

Do not hold back the wages of a hired man overnight.
—Leviticus 19:13 (NIV)

"The check is in the mail" is one of the all-time most frequently told lies. How often do you delay payment for a service rendered? Why? How would you feel if you had to chase down your paycheck?

If someone has done a job for you and there is no dispute about the work done, show him or her appropriate respect, and pay the person promptly.

3

The Way Up Is Down

Surely He scorns the scornful, But gives grace to the humble.
—Proverbs 3:34 (NKJV)

This verse is quoted twice in the New Testament—in James and 1 Peter. Pride often gets in the way of people's relationship with God. The world is full of one-upmanship. People tend to brag about their accomplishments that derive from their abilities. From whom do your abilities come? Rather than being prideful, shouldn't you be grateful for what God provides and give Him the glory?

4

No Time to Waste

Making the most of your time for the days are evil.
—Ephesians 5:16 (NASB)

The most valuable commodity you have on this earth is time. It is especially valuable for at least two reasons. First, when it is gone, no matter how you might try, you cannot gain it back. Second, you have no guarantee how much time you might have. The question is: are you using your time for God's glory or for a lesser purpose?

5
Wisdom of the Ages

But the companion of fools will suffer harm.
—Proverbs 13:20b (NASB)

My father used to say, "You cannot always be in the right place at the right time, but you can figure out the wrong place at the wrong time and make sure you're not there!" Alas, there are some people and some influences you need to avoid. We pray for such when we say, "Lead us not into temptation, but deliver us from evil." The road of life can be rocky and full of holes. You must do your part to stay away from anyone or anything that would cause you to deviate from your walk with Christ!

6
Go On, Kick 'Em while They're Down

You should not look down on your brother in the day of his misfortune.
—Obadiah 12a (NIV)

How often have you remarked, "They got what was coming to them," or "It couldn't have happened to a nicer person"? Take care not to gloat over the calamity that strikes another.

I recall a business deal that seemed to go bad. A church member, chortling, declared, "I just want to know who lost all the money." Why? In such instances, think, *There but for the grace of God go I*. Instead of indulging in smug satisfaction at another's loss, why not pray for him or her instead? We have all been through difficult circumstances. Naturally, we remember those who helped us as well as those who hurt us. What can you do today to help your brother or sister?

Photograph courtesy of Johnny Harris

7

What's Really Important?

The conclusion when all has been heard is: fear God and keep his commandments, because this applies to every person.
—Ecclesiastes 12:13 (NASB)

Have you ever wondered what your purpose was on this earth? Are you to careen along randomly like a pinball, bouncing from one object or event to another? There is a higher purpose! In this context, to fear God means we are to respect, revere, obey, and glorify Him! Without any ambiguity, here is a clear direction. Let us follow it!

8

Something You Can Count On

Jesus Christ is the same yesterday and today, yes and forever.
—Hebrews 13:8 (NASB)

In a chaotic world with perpetual change, isn't it reassuring to have a constant? You can be certain that Jesus will never leave you or forsake you; He is always there for you. He is constant. His Word will remain forever. He was there in the beginning and will never pass away. Can you think of anything as permanent as Jesus Christ?

9
Are You a Busybody?

Make it your ambition to lead a quiet life, to mind your own business and to work with your hands, just as we told you.
—1 Thessalonians 4:11 (NIV)

Oh, how much trouble and strife would be avoided if people followed this verse. Why do humans have such an obsession with the affairs of others? Why do people call attention to themselves? You should strive for a quiet, humble life, and as much as possible, not interfere or become entwined in the affairs of others.

10
How Rich Is Rich Enough?

What good is it for a man to gain the whole world yet forfeit his soul?
—Mark 8:36 (NIV)

No tombstone I have ever seen reads, "I wish I spent more time at the office." Many things vie for prominence in your life. If you allow it, you can be consumed by your career, hobbies, sports, or leisure activities. Why? What about God? Your spouse? Your children? Your extended family? Your friends? Surely these are more important than fleeting riches, fickle fame, or fading pleasure.

11
So You're a Somebody

If anyone thinks he is something when he is nothing, he deceives himself.
—Galatians 6:3 (ESV)

Everyone has known someone who had an inflated sense of self-importance. To brag is the way of the world. As a Christian, you are in the world but not of the world. If ever there was an admonition to humility, here it is! As you grow in Christ, your ego must correspondingly diminish.

Photograph courtesy of Curtis Lewis III

12
Great Expectations

He has told you, o' man, what is good; and what does the Lord require of you but to do justice, and to love kindness and to walk humbly with your God?
—Micah 6:8 (ESV)

I was driving in the north Georgia Mountains and saw Micah 6:8 on a sign as part of the name of a business. When I reached my destination, I read the verse. If you sometimes wonder what God expects of you, here is a concrete answer.

13

Help—Just a Prayer Away

Remember me with favor, O my God.
—Nehemiah 13:31 (NIV)

Have you ever been faced with a situation in which you knew you needed to pray but were unsure what to pray for or how to pray? I bet we all have! This short, simple prayer has been used in a variety of difficult circumstances: "Lord, help!" Try it, and see if the God of heaven won't be stirred to act on your behalf.

14

How to Be Wealthy—Guaranteed!

Bring the whole tithe into the storehouse, that there may be food in my house. Test me in this, says the Lord Almighty, and see if I will throw open the flood gates of heaven and pour out so much blessing that you will not have room enough for it.
—Malachi 3:10 (NIV)

This verse is the only instance I am aware of in which God says to test Him. Clearly, the Lord is serious about tithing! You know if you are really bringing the whole tithe to Him. Be faithful with the tithe, and see what blessings He has in store for you. You will find that you cannot outgive God.

Photograph courtesy of Curtis Lewis III

15
Who Will You Call On?

And it shall come to pass that whoever calls on the name of the Lord will be saved.
—Joel 2:32a (NKJV)

You may recall that this verse from Joel is quoted in the apostle Peter's famous Pentecost sermon recorded in Acts 2. One unusual characteristic of Christianity is inclusivity. It is difficult to become an adherent to many religions; one must be "born into" several. This is not so for the Christian. A Christian can come from any origin or background; our Lord is open to all. We know from John 3:16 that God so loved the world that He gave His Son for us. God loves all of us—the entire world. However, it is up to each individual to call upon Him. You must make the decision to surrender to the Lord. Have you decided?

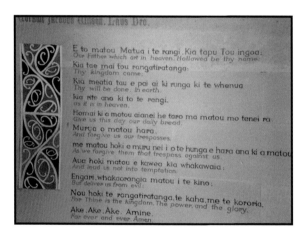

16
There's No Gain without Pain

For we know that all things work together for the good of those who love the Lord and are called according to His purpose.
—Romans 8:28 (NIV)

Sometimes it is difficult to understand how certain things may work for your good. I have often looked back after the passage of time, however, and been very grateful to God about how well things worked out. The Lord's wisdom is markedly superior to human wisdom; He knows what is best for you. You must learn to submit yourself to His will. After all, He is your Father.

17

Don't Gloat Over Another's Misfortune

Men at ease have contempt for misfortune.
—Job 12:5 (NIV)

When you're flying high, you never think it will happen to you—until it happens! What is it? As Job said, that which he had dreaded the most came to pass. He lost his family, health, and wealth. The calamity that strikes is the same in our day. Do not remain aloof from those who suffer, but pray for them, draw near, and befriend them instead.

Photograph courtesy of Johnny Harris

18

Where Does Your Strength Come From?

The Sovereign Lord is my strength.
—Habakkuk 3:19z (NIV)

Many times, I have prayed for strength. Sometimes, I meant physical endurance; at other times, emotional strength was needed. In the book of Philippians, Paul wrote that he could do all things through Christ, who strengthened him. That verse, as well as this one from Habakkuk, tells you about the origin of your strength. Where will you turn when you are spent and need strength?

Photograph courtesy of Brian Dennison

19
How's Your Thinking?

"For my thoughts are not your thoughts, neither are your ways my ways," declares the Lord. "As the heavens are higher than the earth, so are my ways higher than your ways and my thoughts higher than your thoughts."
—Isaiah 55:8–9 (NIV)

Some people reject the Lord, because they cannot understand the Bible. By the same logic, one could deny the law of gravity, since one could not comprehend the science of physics. It is arrogant for people to think they could limit God to their intellect. He is our Creator; certainly, He is on an infinitely higher plane than any person.

20
Wealth Is Forever, Right?

Command those who are rich in this present world not to be arrogant nor put their hope in wealth, which is so uncertain, but to put their hope in God, who richly provides us with everything for our enjoyment.
—1 Timothy 6:17 (NIV)

The world views wealth as the ultimate power. Materialism reigns. However, wealth is fleeting. Embezzlement, an undependable partner, a dramatic market change, or a divorce can quickly dissipate a fortune. The Lord is not affected by the unexpected. I will trust in Him. Will you also trust the Lord?

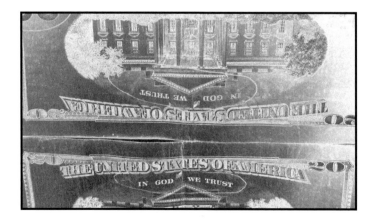

21
Got Doubts?

Be merciful to those who doubt.
—Jude 22 (NIV)

Most people have been doubters at some point in their lives. The Lord is merciful to those who doubt. In fact, He is patient, desiring that all come to know Him. We should, likewise, be patient and kindhearted in our witness to those whom God puts in our paths! What can you do to lead someone to the Lord?

22
Where Is Home for You?

For our citizenship is in heaven, from which also we eagerly wait for a Savior, the Lord Jesus Christ.
—Philippians 3:20 (NASB)

You may have friends who get very upset about political events, government incompetence, and the like. Why do they get so upset? We are just passing through this earth. Keep your eye on the prize (as Paul said), and remember where your true citizenship lies!

Photograph courtesy of Eleanor Eades, MD

23

Wimp or Warrior—Which Are You?

For if you remain silent at this time, relief and deliverance will arise for the Jews from another place and you and your father's house will perish. And who knows whether you have not attained royalty for such a time as this?
—Esther 4:14 (NASB)

Esther had been chosen as Queen of Persia, and in such a position, she was asked by her kinsman, Mordecai, to go before the king on behalf of the Jews. She was hesitant, as she was afraid.

We can learn from this episode. No one should shrink from the duty God has called him or her to do. The position you are in or the talent you possess has been given to you by Him, and He has a purpose you need to fulfill. Are you using your gifts to fulfill God's purpose today?

24

Have I Got Plans For You!

"For I know the plans that I have for you," declares the Lord, "plans to prosper you and not to harm you, plans to give you a hope and a future."
—Jeremiah 29:11 (NIV)

The Lord has planned for your best interest. Just as a father wants the best for his child, so does the Lord desire the best for us.

My daughter was afraid when I took her to school on her first day. However, I knew the plan I had for her education and that she was at the right place. Likewise, the Lord knows the plan He has for you and the blessings you will receive. Ask Him to reveal His plan to you and so lead you.

25
Who Will You Serve?

But as for me and my household, we will serve the Lord.
—Joshua 24:15b (NIV)

You must determine that you will serve God regardless of what others may do. You must not be swayed by the actions of others. Your relationship with the risen Christ is of the utmost importance. As the old song says, "I have decided to follow Jesus ... though none go with me; still I will follow!"

26
Don't Become the Devil's Dinner

Be sober, be vigilant; because your adversary the devil walks about like a roaring lion, seeking whom he may devour.
—1 Peter 5:8 (NKJV)

The Devil is delighted when you underestimate him. Make no mistake—he is alive and active. In fact, he is the prince of this earthly world. He constantly does harm in a myriad of subtle ways—the various temptations that arise, the small things that anger you or cause you to worry, or your rationalization of sinful acts. Be alert! Stand up to him, call on the name of Jesus, and the Devil will flee!

Photograph courtesy of Brian Dennison

27
Always Do Good

Therefore to one who knows the right thing to do and does not do it, to him it is sin.
—James 4:17 (NASB)

Have you ever regretted a missed opportunity? We all have! Seize the opportunity to do good for others, be a blessing, and glorify God. Do not become a sinner of omission!

28
Look Before You Leap

Suppose one of you wants to build a tower. Will he not first sit down and estimate the cost to see if he has enough money to complete it.
—Luke 14:28 (NIV)

You have probably known people who are impulsive, who go into something half-cocked. Both Scripture and prudence dictate that we carefully consider our actions before proceeding. Lord knows, if you take this advice, it will save you a lot of grief.

29
Slow Down; Take a Closer Look

Grace to you and peace from God our father and the Lord Jesus Christ.
—Philemon 3 (NIV)

Many times, I have hurried though this verse and others like it, taking it for granted as sort of a stock greeting. When I slowed down my reading, however, I gained a new appreciation for it. The grace refers to the gift of salvation we have received. This peace was promised to us by Jesus in John 14. Be thankful for them both!

Photograph courtesy of Johnny Harris

30
Fault-Finding

Therefore let us not judge one another anymore, but rather resolve this, not to put a stumbling block or a cause to fall in our brother's way.
—Romans 14:13 (NIV)

It is easy and tempting to point out the faults of others. The harder thing to do is to keep watch on yourself so that you do not lead another astray by your words or deeds. It can be difficult to stay on the right road. Is there a stumbling block you need to remove? What are you doing to lead people *to* the Lord?

31
Give It All You've Got

Whatever you do, work at it with all your heart, as working for the Lord, not for men, since you know that you will receive an inheritance from the Lord as a reward. It is the Lord Jesus you are serving.
—Colossians 3:23–24 (NIV)

Booker T. Washington said, "If a job is worth doing; it is worth doing right." You should also be very conscientious, as you do not work for other people but for the Lord. Let your work—whatever it may be, however menial it may seem—be done with excellence so that it brings honor and glory to the Lord.

32
Give Me Mercy, Not Justice

For God did not send his Son into the world to condemn the world, but to save the world through him.
—John 3:17 (NIV)

Most Christians are familiar with John 3:16, but how many know by heart the verse that follows? My childhood Sunday school teacher, Mary Donohue, did, and she stressed it. Mercy triumphs over judgment. God is merciful to you. Proving that, He sent His Son not to judge you but to redeem you!

33
Wounds of a Friend

Faithful are the wounds of a friend, but the kisses of an enemy are deceitful.
—Proverbs 27:6 (KJV)

All people like to hear the positives about themselves, but beware the flattery of others. A true friend will hold you accountable and kindly point out that which you need to correct.

34
Loose Lips Sink Ships

He who guards his mouth and his tongue keeps himself from calamity.
—Proverbs 21:23 (NIV)

We can avoid a whole lot of trouble by following this advice. As Will Rogers once said, "It's a whole lot easier not to let the cat out of the bag than to put him back once he's out." Think before you speak, because once you have spoken, you can't take what you said back!

35
A Faithful Witness

In everything set them an example by doing what is good. In your teaching show integrity, seriousness and soundness of speech, that cannot be condemned, so that those who oppose you may be ashamed because they have nothing bad to say about us.
—Titus 2:7–8 (NIV)

You should always consider your words and deeds carefully for the effect they may have. Christians are to glorify God. You should not let it be said that you have done anything less. Mahatma Gandhi reportedly said, "I love your Christ; it is your Christians I do not like." Do not detract from Christ's glory.

Photograph courtesy of Johnny Harris

36
Is Trouble Headed Your Way?

The Lord is good, a refuge in times of trouble. He cares for those who trust in Him.
—Nahum 1:7 (NIV)

When trouble comes upon you (and it most certainly will), you have the assurance that the Lord is there with you. He will deliver you—if not from the trouble, then through the trouble, whatever it may be. Who is your refuge?

37
The Fiery Trial

If we are thrown into the blazing furnace, the God we serve is able to save us from it, and He will rescue us from your hand O King. But even if He does not, we want you to know O King that we will not serve your gods or worship the image of gold you have set up.
—Daniel 3:17–18 (NIV)

When King Nebuchadnezzar erected a gold idol and ordered all in his kingdom to bow before it, three men refused. Shadrach, Meshach, and Abednego stated they would not worship an idol but only serve God, even if it meant death. Let nothing come between God and you; serve the risen Lord. He is the Rock of your salvation.

38
Got Knowledge and Wisdom?

All scripture is God-breathed and is useful for teaching, rebuking, correcting and training in righteousness so that the man of God may be thoroughly equipped for every good work.
—2 Timothy 3:16–17 (NIV)

Many times, I have found a new inspiration or understanding in a verse I had previously read many times. The Word of God trains us to be men and women of God. You could receive no greater compliment than to be so called.

39
Fear or Faith—Your Choice

Have I not commanded you? Be strong and of good courage; do not be afraid, nor be dismayed, for the Lord your God is with you wherever you go.
—Joshua 1:9 (NIV)

Faith is stronger than fear. Therefore, replace fear with faith, and see what happens.

While traveling in Costa Rica, I heard a sermon which addressed this issue. The minister repeatedly stated that nothing is secure. He made the point that people think security will free them from fear, but since nothing on this earth is secure, this reasoning is flawed. The take home message for me was that only faith in the Lord would overcome fear.

40
How's Your Thought Life?

We compel every human thought to surrender to obedience to Christ.
—2 Corinthians 10:56 (NEB)

Have you ever had thoughts you did not want but were recurring—thoughts that were detrimental to you and that you knew were contrary to the will of God? I certainly have. I am grateful to the minister who shared this verse with me. Through the power of Christ, you can banish unholy thoughts. Concentrate on godly thoughts and ideas.

41
The Real Deal

But do not trust any and every spirit, my friends; test the spirits, to see whether they are from God.
—1 John 4:1a (NEB)

We live in a fallen world, and the Devil seeks to deceive us and separate us from the love of Christ. You must use caution and pray for guidance. John went on to say that "every spirit which acknowledges that Jesus Christ has come in the flesh is from God" (1 John 4:2).

42
Cut Down or Build Up?

Whenever Hannah went up to the house of the Lord, her rival provoked her till she wept and would not eat.
—1 Samuel 1:7b (NIV)

Humans can be very cruel to one another. The caustic remarks and harsh words people use can cut another to the quick. Consider carefully what you say. Build others up; do not tear them down.

43

Obedient Servants of God

And this is love, that we walk according to His commandments. This is the commandment, just as you have heard from the beginning that you should walk in it.
—2 John 6 (NASB)

We know what the commands of God are; He has given us His Word so we will know. We know He loves us, as He gave His only Son, Jesus, to die for our sins. Show your love for Him and others by keeping His commandments! Remember, actions speak louder than words.

44

Cold or Hot—Which Are You?

So then, because you are lukewarm and neither cold nor hot, I will spew you out of my mouth.
—Revelation 3:16 (NKJV)

Do you just go through the motions as you practice your faith? You need to rise to the occasion; you should be on fire for the Lord. Oswald Chambers put it well: "Remember what you are saved for—that the Son of God might be manifested in your mortal flesh."

45
Right Thinking

Finally, brethren, whatever things are true, whatever things are noble, whatever things are just, whatever things are pure, whatever things are lovely, whatever things are of good report, if there is any virtue and if there is anything praiseworthy—meditate on these things.
—Philippians 4:8 (NKJV)

Proverbs 23:7 teaches that "as a man thinketh in his heart so is he." Consequently, train your thoughts to be pleasing to God. When you cultivate the habit of pure and pleasant thought, you will be amazed how much strength you have to resist worry, envy, pride, anxiety, and temptation.

46
Seeking God's Best

Seek good and not evil, that you may live; and thus may the Lord God of hosts be with you, just as you have said!
—Amos 5:14 (NASB)

You may have heard the blessing, "The Lord be with you." Sin (evil) separates people from God. Jesus paid the penalty for that sin. Do what is pleasing to God (seek good), and avoid anything that would hinder your close relationship with Him!

After I took the photograph below of this Spanish shepherd with his flock, he said to me, "*Vaya con Dios.*" We should always aspire to follow that shepherd's advice and " go with God".

47

Godly Examples

My dear friend, do not imitate bad examples, but good ones. The well-doer is a child of God; the evil-doer has never seen God.
—3 John 11 (NEB)

You have seen bad examples. Do not let that be said of you. Christians are not only followers of Christ, but also representatives of Him. You may be the only example of Christianity that another person experiences. Let your example be pleasing in His sight!

48

Who Do You Follow?

But Ruth said "Do not urge me to leave you or turn back from following you; for where you go, I will go and where you lodge, I will lodge. Your people shall be my people and your God, my God."
—Ruth 1:16 (NASB)

Ruth left her homeland and the people and culture she knew not just to follow her mother-in-law, Naomi, but much more importantly, to also follow God. Following the Lord may be difficult at times, but you must obey His will. If you follow the Lord, He will be faithful and care for you, just as He did for Ruth. Will you surrender to the Lord and follow His path?

49
Practice Makes Perfect!

For Ezra had set his heart to study the law of the Lord, and to practice it.
—Ezra 7:10a (NASB)

It is not enough to know the teaching of the Lord; you are called to put it into practice. In the book of James, we learn that faith without works is dead. Do not be passive, but actively demonstrate your faith in everyday living. Do you put into practice what you study?

50
Doing Your Own Thing

In those days Israel had no King; everyone did as he saw fit.
—Judges 21:25 (NIV)

Humans are depraved creatures. People are not capable of self-direction. Humans suffer from tunnel vision and are blind to much of what is around. When people do as they see fit, then sin, misery, and chaos ensue. The most cursory review of history will confirm this fact. The late, great country music star, Waylon Jennings, sang, "I've been ridin' these highways; been doin' things my way and it's makin' me lonesome, ornery, and mean." Does that sound familiar? It doesn't have to be that way. Christians have a king—King Jesus. When you surrender to the King and He directs your life, you will experience purpose, order, and above all, joy.

51

Are You a Peacemaker?

Blessed are the peacemakers, for they will be called sons of God.
—Matthew 5:9 (NIV)

I heard a minister make the point that this world has an abundance of troublemakers but very few peacemakers. He went on to say that we have the peacemaker in our hearts. Be careful not to become embroiled in turmoil. Instead, exert a positive witness by striving for harmony and peace in your relationships.

Painting by Emile Munier, photograph courtesy of Kim Iocovozzi

52

What Are You Reaping?

As I have observed, those who plow evil and those who sow trouble reap it.
—Job 4:8 (NIV)

The people described in this verse would be the opposite of peacemakers. Jesus said, "Blessed are the peacemakers." There is no blessing for those who plow evil and sow trouble. Carefully consider your actions and what consequences may follow.

53
Time Out to Rest

Remember the Sabbath day by it keeping it holy.
—Exodus 20:8 (NIV)

God knows very well that people need a day to rest from labor. On that day, you should devote yourself to Him with thanksgiving, praise, reflection, and study of His Word. Avoid working to catch up or get ahead so you can concentrate on what is most important—your relationship with the Lord. How will you spend your day of rest?

Photograph courtesy of Brian Dennison

54
Who Do You Trust?

The Lord is good to those whose hope is in Him, to the one who seeks him.
—Lamentations 3:25 (NIV)

Is your hope truly in the Lord? If you put your hope or trust in someone or something other than the Lord, it is misplaced, and you will be disappointed. Consider carefully the various people and things you have trusted in the past. Have any of them failed you?

55
You Can Run, But You Can't Hide!

And you can be sure that your sin will find you out.
—Numbers 32:23 (NIV)

These words were originally spoken to the tribes of Reuben and Gad as they settled on the other side of the Jordan River. However, they are certainly applicable to Christians today. Sin always has consequences. Although you have forgiveness through the Lord Jesus Christ, the consequences of your sin can be very painful to you and others. It is best to pray for strength to avoid temptation and sin in the first place.

56
I've Got Your Back

But the Lord is to be trusted, and he will fortify you and guard you from the evil one.
—2 Thessalonians 3:3 (NEB)

The great German theologian, Martin Luther, described the Lord as a mighty fortress. Luther knew all too well that this world is the Devil's domain and hence hostile territory for the believer. However, our trust is in the Lord, and He will strengthen and protect us. After all, we pray from the prayer Jesus taught the disciples, "Deliver us from evil"(Matthew 6:13).

57
What Do You Worship?

Those who cling to worthless idols forfeit the grace that could be theirs.
—Jonah 2:8 (NIV)

What idols come between you and the grace the Lord has given you—money, sports, vanity, sex? These carnal idols have no lasting value; they are indeed worthless. The Lord will never tarnish, devalue, age out, or fail to perform. Put aside worthless idols, and choose everlasting value.

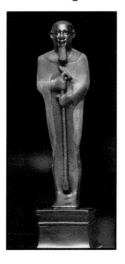

Photograph courtesy of Wasil Khan, MD, PhD.

58
Hey, Look at Me!

You may say to yourself, "My power and the strength of my hands have produced this wealth for me." But remember the Lord your God, for it is he who gives you the ability to produce wealth, and so confirms his covenant, which he swore to your forefathers, as it is this day.
—Deuteronomy 8:17 (NIV)

You may say to yourself, *Look at me and what I have achieved!* Surely all have thought it at one time or another. If you are honest with yourself and God, you will soon realize that you can achieve very little on your own. As Jesus said, "Apart from me you can do nothing"(John 15:5). Give credit where credit is due! Instead of basking in your own perceived glory, remember to thank God for the gifts and abilities He has given you.

Photograph courtesy of Chip McDaniel

59
Forget Me Not

If you ever forget the Lord your God and follow other gods and worship and bow down to them, I testify against you today that you will surely be destroyed.
—Deuteronomy 8:19 (NIV)

When you remember the Lord and follow Him, life has meaning, direction, and fulfillment. Anything that you focus on more than God becomes another god. Do not allow anything to rival your devotion to God. This even applies to your own family (Matthew 10:37). If you do so, you precipitate your own destruction. Is there anything coming between you and God?

60
Forging Ahead

And the priests who carried the ark of the covenant of the Lord stood firm on dry ground in the middle of the Jordan while all Israel crossed on dry ground, until the nation had finished crossing the Jordan.
—Joshua 3:17 (NASB)

The great Jamaican musician, Jimmy Cliff, had a massive hit entitled "Many Rivers to Cross." We all face many obstacles in life—rivers we must ford. The Israelites were led by the Ark of the Covenant of the Lord when they successfully crossed the Jordan River. If you seek the Lord's guidance and follow Him, you will successfully cross the many rivers in your journey through this life. What obstacles do you face? Have you asked the Lord for His help and guidance in dealing with them?

61
On the Same Page

Do two men walk together unless they have made an appointment (or agreement)?
—Amos 3:3 (NASB)

People use many analogies for the Christian life. One commonly employed is "the Christian walk" or "walking with the Lord." As Amos taught, that walk will not transpire unless an appointment or agreement has been made. Some might use the word *commitment* or *surrender* to describe that agreement. Have you made that appointment or agreement with the Lord? Do you follow the Lord's path?

62
Listening for God

So He said, "Go forth and stand on the mountain before the Lord." And behold the Lord was passing by! And a great and strong wind was rending the mountains and breaking in pieces the rocks before the Lord; but the Lord was not in the wind. And after the wind an earthquake, but the Lord was not in the earthquake. And after the earthquake a fire, but the Lord was not in the fire; and after the fire a sound of a gentle blowing. And it came about when Elijah heard it, that he wrapped his face in his mantle, and went out and stood in the entrance of the cave. And behold, a voice came to him and said, "What are you doing here, Elijah?"
—1 Kings 19:11–13 (NASB)

Do you expect a momentous happening to herald the Lord's communication with you? Are you willing to be still and listen for the voice from the gentle blowing?

63

The Whole Truth, and Nothing but the Truth

These are the things ye shall do; speak ye every man the truth to his neighbor; execute the judgment of truth and peace in your gates: And let none of you imagine evil in your hearts against his neighbor; and love no false oath; for all these are things that I hate saith the Lord.
—Zechariah 8:16 (KJV)

Truth has become a casualty of human societal development. Truth was once acknowledged as absolute; now it is considered relative. Yet that is not how the Lord views truth. Anything less than the truth or a deviation from the truth is false. The Lord detests falsehoods. Remember, He gave a commandment not to lie. Do you obey that commandment?

64

Anxiety Pill

So he answered, "Do not fear, for those who are with us are more than those who are with them."
—2 Kings 6:16 (NASB)

This sentence was spoken by Elisha as an answer to his servant's anxiety upon seeing that the city of Dothan was surrounded by the Arameans. Next, Elisha asked the Lord to open his servant's eyes. The Lord did so, and the servant saw that there were horses and chariots of fire all around. Subsequently, the Arameans were struck with blindness, and the threat to Elisha was removed.

Remember that the Lord is with you, and you do not need to be afraid. Perhaps you should pray that He will open your eyes as He did for the servant of Elisha.

Photograph courtesy of Brian Dennison

65
To Forgive

When Joseph's brothers saw that their father was dead, they said, "Perhaps Joseph will hate us, and may actually repay us for all the evil which we did to him." So they sent messengers to Joseph, saying, "Before your father died he commanded, saying, 'Thus you shall say to Joseph; "I beg you, please forgive the trespass of your brothers and their sin; for they did evil to you." "Now, please forgive the trespass of the servants of the God of your father." And Joseph wept when they spoke to him. Then his brothers also went and fell down before his face, and they said, "Behold we are your servants."
Joseph said to them, "Do not be afraid, for am I in the place of God? But as for you, you meant evil against me; but God meant it for good, in order to bring it about as it is this day, to save many people alive."
—Genesis 50:15–20 (NKJV)

Joseph's brothers had sold him into slavery; yet the Lord raised him to a position of power in Egypt, second only to Pharaoh. A time came when his brothers needed food and went to Egypt for grain. Joseph forgave them and reunited the family.

Forgiving can be very difficult, especially among family members. Many people carry the burden of resentment over some prior hurtful act for years. Perhaps that is why holiday family gatherings can be so stressful. Joseph had much to forgive, and he set a great example. Do likewise, and forgive those who have wronged you. Jesus said in Matthew 6:14–15, "If you forgive men their trespasses, your heavenly Father will also forgive you but if you do not forgive men their trespasses, neither will your Father forgive your trespasses."

66
I Saw It with My Own Eyes

For I delivered to you as of first importance what I also received, that Christ died for our sins according to the scriptures and that He was buried, and that He was raised on the third day according to the scriptures, and that He appeared to Cephas, then to the twelve. After that He appeared to more than five hundred brethren at one time, most of whom remain until now, but some have fallen asleep; then He appeared to James, then to all the apostles; and last of all as if to one untimely born, He appeared to me also.
—1 Corinthians 15:3–8 (NASB)

These few short verses summarize a Christian's beliefs and provide a list of witnesses to the resurrection. It is thought that this portion of 1 Corinthians represents an early church creed preceding the Nicene and Apostles Creeds by centuries. Does this portion of Scripture represent your belief?

67

Have You Lost Your Way?

Be still and know that I am God; I will be exalted among the nations, I will be exalted in the earth.
—Psalm 46:10 (NIV)

As you proceed through the tumult and shouting of life, you sometimes lose your bearings. Rather than drifting along, you need to consult your compass—the Lord. Pause, and recognize His majesty and control. Then follow Him.

Photograph courtesy of Chip McDaniel

68

Trouble, Trouble Everywhere

In this world you will have trouble, but take heart, I have overcome the world.
—John 16:33b (NIV)

Many people assume that the Christian's life should be free from difficulty. Jesus actually stated the contrary. A friend once pointed out to me that the Lord does not always deliver us from trouble, but He will deliver us through trouble. Deliverance through our trials is an opportunity for spiritual growth. Pray for the ability to recognize the opportunity rather than merely focus on the trouble.

Photograph courtesy of Curtis Lewis III

69
Trials and Tribulations

"We must go through many hardships to enter the kingdom of God," they said.
—Acts 14:22b (NIV)

These words were spoken by Paul and Barnabas to the believers in Lystra, Iconium, and Antioch. Do not expect life to be without difficulty because you are a Christian. In fact, throughout the New Testament, we are told that we will face trials. Jesus said that people would revile His followers. Consider the calamities Paul experienced: shipwreck, imprisonment, beatings, a stoning, etc. The book of James states that the testing of your faith develops perseverance. Remember that the Lord is with you through hard times.

70
Misguided Trust

If I tell the righteous man that he will surely live, but then he trusts in his righteousness and does evil, none of the righteous things he has done will be remembered; he will die for the evil he has done.
—Ezekiel 33:13 (NIV)

Many people have the belief that if they do more good deeds than bad in life, that will somehow get them into heaven. Contrary to that view, Romans 3:23 states that "all have sinned and fall short of the glory of God." If your righteousness could attain salvation, why would Christ have died to pay the penalty of your sin? Trusting in your own righteousness is misplaced trust. Therefore, you must properly place your trust in God.

71
Pride Comes Before a Fall

Seek the Lord, all you humble of the land, you who do what he commands. Seek righteousness, seek humility; perhaps you will be sheltered on the day of the Lord's anger.
—Zephaniah 2:3 (NIV)

Christians tend to strive toward righteousness, but do you seek to be humble? Frequently quoted from Proverbs 16:18 is the old adage, "Pride goes before destruction." Pride gets in the way of your relationship with the Lord. Many are too proud to fully surrender to Him, to turn not just their troubles, but also their entire lives over to Him. Instead of demonstrating pride, you should practice humbling yourself. Will you bow before the Lord today?

72
How Do You Measure Up?

Noah did everything just as God commanded him.
—Genesis 6:22 (NIV)

This short verse summarizes the faithfulness of Noah. Doing everything "just as God commanded him" was no easy task for Noah. He built an enormous ark, assembled a multitude of animals, and cared for them—all while waiting for the flood. Do you do everything just as God commanded? His commandments are clear; they are recorded in Scripture. Show your love for the Lord by following His commandments. How do you measure up compared to the example set by Noah?

73

Prayer—Your First Port of Call?

In the thirty-ninth year of his reign, Asa was afflicted with a disease in his feet. Though his disease was severe, even in his illness he did not seek help from the Lord, but only from the physicians.
—2 Chronicles 16:12 (NIV)

I recall a time several years ago when I was in Barbados and a young woman working at the hotel confided in me about a problem she was facing. When I asked if she had prayed about it, she looked at me in dismay. Then she responded that she had not, but maybe she should. I agreed.

How much grief do you needlessly bear when you try to go it alone? Why not follow the advice of the old hymn and take it to the Lord in prayer?

74

Are You Missing Out?

And David was unwilling to move the ark of the Lord into the city of David with him; but David took it aside to the house of Obed-Edom the Gittite ... Now it was told King David, saying "The Lord has blessed the house of Obed-Edom and all that belongs to him, on account of the ark of God." And David went and brought up the ark of God from the house of Obed-Edom into the city of David with gladness.
—2 Samuel 6:10, 12 (NASB)

When David learned of the blessings that accrued for the man who housed the ark of the Lord, he changed his mind and had the ark brought into the city in which he lived. How many blessings do you miss out on because you shut the Lord out your home or other areas of your life?

75

Who Is the Light of Your Life?

For you are my lamp, O Lord, and my God lightens my darkness.
—2 Samuel 22:29 (ESV)

Most people trudge through life with no direction, purpose, or plan. Instead, they simply react to events as they occur. If you surrender your life to the Lord, He will guide you, lead you, and give you direction! Which would you prefer—groping along in the darkness or the Lord illuminating the way?

76

How Tight Is Your Grip?

But who am I, and what is my people that we should be able to offer this willingly? For all things come from you and of your own have we given you.
—1 Chronicles 29:14 (ESV)

I was curious about the inherent meaning of a minister's repeated offertory prayer. He habitually asked God's blessing on "Your tithes and our offerings." I came to realize that the tithe already belonged to God, and we merely gave it back via our offerings. When you consider that your wealth is all His anyway, shouldn't you be generous in your offering? After all, the Lord allows money and possessions to merely pass through your hands; when you die, someone else will claim them!

77

Is Your Faith Half-Baked?

Ephraim is a flat cake not turned over.
—Hosea 7:8b (NIV)

An Anglican minister once gave a great illustration to help me better understand this verse. He spoke of a pancake being cooked only on one side so that it was burned on the cooked side and still full of gooey batter on the upper side. Obviously, such a pancake would not be edible. The people of Ephraim (the dominant tribe of Israel in Hosea's day) separated their religion from secular life so that there was really no manifestation of religion in their lives. Do you compartmentalize life such that you prevent your light from shining? Others should see your devotion to Christ—not just on Sunday at church, but also throughout your life day by day.

78

How Strong Is Love?

Many waters cannot quench love; rivers cannot wash it away. If one were to give all the wealth of his house for love, it would be utterly scorned.
—Song of Songs 8:7 (NIV)

Nothing on this earth is stronger than love. No matter how one might try, love cannot be extinguished. Love cannot be purchased. Perhaps the strongest love we humans can comprehend is that of a parent for his or her child. God's love for you is so profound that He gave His only Son for you. Can you imagine sacrificing the life of your loved one so someone else could live?

CPSIA information can be obtained
at www.ICGtesting.com
Printed in the USA
LVIC06n1329061113

360243LV00006B/12